Shock and Aw!

Lotus Collection

This edition first published in 2003
The Lotus Collection
An imprint of
Roli Books Pvt. Ltd.
M-75, G.K. II Market
New Delhi 110 048
Phones: ++91 (011) 2921 2271, 2921 2782
2921 0886, Fax: ++91 (011) 2921 7185
E-mail: roli@vsnl.com; Website: rolibooks.com
Also at
Varanasi, Agra, Jaipur and the Netherlands

ISBN: 81-7436-270-3
Rs 99

Typeset in Imperium by Roli Books Pvt. Ltd. and
printed at Sheel Print N Pack, Noida.

'There's no question that the minute I got elected, the storm clouds on the horizon were getting nearly directly overhead.'

'I know what I believe. I will continue to articulate what I believe and what I believe—I believe that what I believe is right.'

'When I'am talking about—when I'm talking about myself, and when he's talking about myself, all of us are talking about me.'

—George W. Bush

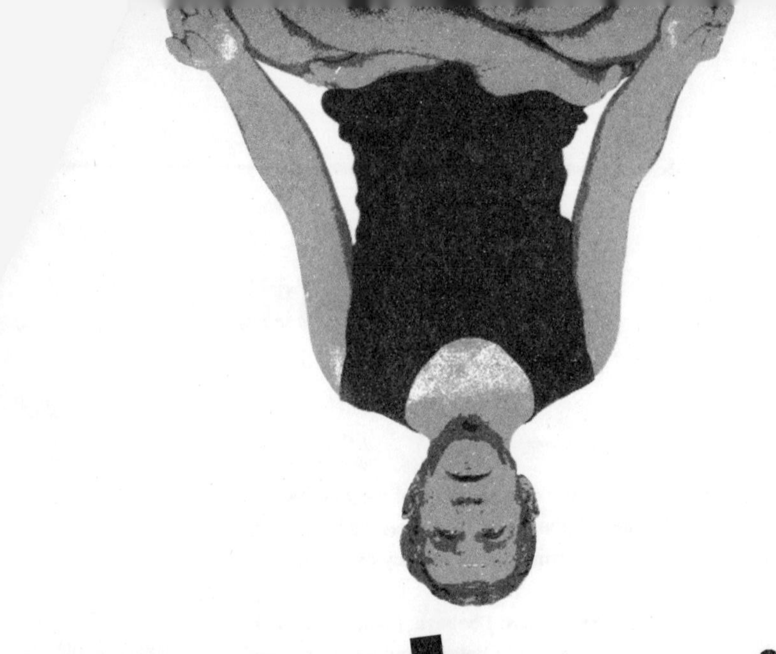

Shock and joke book

Foreplay **Suhel Seth**

LOTUS COLLECTION
ROLI BOOKS

Foreplay

An interview with George W. Bush, the 43rd President of the United States of America

The interview is conducted at The Oval Office in The White House. The rug has been replaced with a thick carpet, which now bears the face of Saddam Hussein. Guests are invited to stamp his face and clean their soles around Saddam's eyes!

Suhel Seth: Good morning, Mr President. It is indeed very kind of you to see me. I am from Delhi.

Bush: Ah, how's the weather in Delhi? California must be hot now. Isn't nothing like Texas.

Seth: Mr President I am from Delhi, India not Delhi, California.

Bush: Ah, the land of Gandhi. Pity she was shot. And her husband too! Terrorism ah!

Seth: Actually, Mr President, in our country almost every Gandhi has been shot but I guess you are referring to Indira and her son Rajiv Gandhi. But there is a more famous Gandhi: Mahatma Gandhi.

Bush: Of course, read a lot about him. The guy's got a great body. Must have been a regular at the gym. So Mr Delhi, oh, Mr Seth, what can I do for you this morning?

Seth: Mr President, we in India are very

concerned about this unfair war on Iraq and we believe there must have been another way for this to end?

Bush: Aw sure, no kidding. No kidding. We could have waited for another four years for the United Nations to move its ass. What would I have told my Dad and Jeff? How would I have avenged family honour? How would I have gone back to my ranch and told all the staff there that I ain't gonna do what they all thought I was gonna do??? Eh??? Saddam was or perhaps is or perhaps we don't know, a monster. Monsters need to go. The Bible says that. We in the United States are committed to getting the world rid of all monsters. Saddam was one and he gotta go. The only problem is we don't know where he's gone. But I am sure Tommy will find him. This is the smoking gun White House my friend. We smoke all these folks and we do it with ease and precision. We smoke them and then we extinguish them. Ha, ha...

Seth: But Mr President people are saying you went to Afghanistan and couldn't find Bin Laden; you went to Iraq and you can't find Saddam. What are your views?

Bush: Look my Indian friend, this ain't no silly war that you guys keep having with that General fellow. This is serious stuff. It's very difficult to find chaps like Bin Laden and

Saddam and even they know that. Which is why I am now planning to attack Syria and then Iran and then Namibia and then perhaps Haiti till we can find Saddam. I am committed to making these terrorist folks suffer and I've told anyone who cares to listen that I want these folks either dead or alive!

Seth: But isn't this an excuse for attacking all countries you don't like? Or perhaps don't agree with you?

Bush: Not at all. We gotta keep going to war until we can find Laden and Saddam. Till then, we in the United States shall not rest. It is my Biblical duty and I shall do it. No matter how much time it takes. Donald, Dick, Tommy and I are no push-overs and the world be warned!

Seth: But aren't you violating norms of international decency? Of international diplomacy?

Bush: Look here we folks have gotta a job to do and we intend doing it. This war on terror shall continue till we find these two fellas. All of us are committed to it. Decency and Diplomacy are the two Ds we ain't following. Ha, ha, ha. Liked that???

Seth: But what if these people are dead? Who will you then find?

Bush: Hey you guys think we are silly? How many people have we named on that deck of cards in Iraq? 55. Get it? 55. We ain't resting till each of those 55 is found. That should give us a pretty long span of time to do what we want to do. The United States is the world's most powerful country and these oil slickers in the Middle East better realize that. The earlier, the better.

Seth: Mr President, the other criticism is that you are after their oil; their reconstruction projects and basically their money. Not their liberation.

Bush: Listen, I know what I am doing. Get it? I know what I am doing. Oil is not just for America. It's for you, for that General who lives across you; for my friend Tony; for that silly bugger Chirac: it's for everyone. We ain't just after oil. We are after everything. See what we did to their museum. We will now make Iraq feel as young a country as the United States. It will no longer be the land of Babylon and the Karbala. We are going to get these guys going. McDonalds and Pizza Hut are already looking at site plans. Coca Cola is setting up bottling plants and I have convinced Madonna to do a show there praising Allah. It's all coming together. Like I said it would. All of it. And believe it or not, Dad and Jeff are so happy. I am fighting for family values. What do you guys in India fight for?

Seth: We barely have the strength to fight for anything after we have finished fighting for water and electricity! Do you sleep peacefully at night? Don't pictures of war haunt you?

Bush: I am telling you, we in the United States are lucky to have pharmacy companies that are almost always dealing with depression. I have no issues with sleep at all. Laura and I go to bed just after 9 p.m. after the last cartoon on CNN is aired and we wake up at 6 a.m. to hymns on peace. It's a great feeling Seth. Great taking care of the world. One day you must sleep with me. It is truly tremendous.

Seth: Finally, Mr President, how would you like to be remembered?

Bush: Gee, that's a tough one. Hey, you got me on that one! But I guess I want to be remembered as a President who may have won in weird circumstances but never ever lost a war. As a man who took on the mightiest in the world. A man who smoked chaps who created trouble; who dug deep into their evil holes and took them out. The gravedigger of terrorists... ha,ha... like Bin Laden and Saddam and made them grovel. Once they were found that is. As a man who avenged the humiliation meted out to his Dad. By the way, do you like this carpet??? As a man who was bright enough to show the world, the light at the end of a really long and horrible tunnel. As George Dubya who never had any doubt. Ha, that was clever eh???

Seth: Thank you ever so much.

Bush: Laura, get Seth and me that burger Mum made. And add some chillies for this Indian friend of mine. India is a great country. Give my respect to those Gandhi fellas. By the way, which one of them is running your country now? Tell them if they need any help, just call me and we'll be there with all our boys. Liberate you from anything you wish. Just don't get us involved with water and electricity. We first gotta get Baghdad going!

— by Suhel Seth

Note: All George W. Bush quotes are in bold.

Just Bush

What's the difference between God and Bush?—God doesn't believe he's Bush!

Why won' t Bush get into a midlife crisis?—Because he will never leave puberty behind him!

After the war, Bush is going to divide Iraq into three zones: normal, super and unleaded.

Dubya is inaugurating the Olympics. He takes out the paper with his speech and starts reading, 'Zero, zero, zero, zero, zero.' One of his councillors whispers to him, 'Mr President, you have just read out the Olympic rings.'

WASHINGTON (Reuters) A tragic fire on Monday destroyed the personal library of President George W. Bush. Both of his books have been lost.

Presidential spokesperson Ari Fleischer said the President was devastated, as he had not finished coloring the second one.

When a reporter asked Bush what he thought about his first hundred days in office he replied: 'Has it been a year already?'

Bush was in court, charged with parking his car in a restricted area. The judge asked him if he had anything to say in his defence.

'They should not put up such misleading notices,' Bush said, peeved. 'The sign clearly said: FINE FOR PARKING HERE.'

Three sharks meet in the ocean. They talk about the people they have eaten recently. The first one says: 'I swallowed the Ayatollah yesterday, but the guy had eaten so much garlic I still feel sick.' The second shark says: 'That's nothing pal! I swallowed Boris Yeltsin last week and the old guy had so much vodka in him that I'm still drunk.' The third shark laughs and says: 'You lucky guys! I swallowed George W. Bush three weeks ago and the guy has so much air in his head, I still can't dive!'

Bush thinks the thesaurus is a character from *Jurassic Park 3.*

Japanese Prime Minister Koizumi gave Dubya a Bonsai tree. Bush says, 'Not bad, buddy. But back in Texas we've got Bonsai trees a thousand times bigger than this.'

Bush proposed a toast to his favourite people, 'The Japanesians.'

Bush Junior and Bush Senior are on board a small two-seater plane when suddenly Bush Sr., the pilot, parachutes out of the plane. Not knowing how to fly a plane, National Guard Service or not, Bush Jr. grabs the radio.

'Mayday, mayday, my dad just jumped out of the plane.'

Ground control receives the call and replies.

'Your dad?'

'He left me here, took the parachute.'

'Sir, your dad?'

'He is the pilot, gosh!'

'Ok, don't worry, sir. I'll talk you down. Just do as I say. First, I need you to give me your height and position.'

'I'm over six feet and sitting in the front.'

Senior Junior I

'Those are two hyporhetorical questions.'

–George Bush Senior

'I've got a record, a record that is conservative and a record that is compassionated.'

–George W. Bush

Bush comes to India for the first time

...and was taken to a hotel. Bush had a hearty meal and then went to wash his hands but began washing the basin instead. The manager came running on seeing the President, surrounded by a thick black cordon of his Secret Service bodyguards, around the washbasin. 'What are you doing, Sir?' he asked with evident consternation.

Bush gave the manager a cold Presidential stare and replied, 'Don't confuse matters. Haven't you written, "Wash Basin" on the board.'

...and was coming down Raisina Hill after seeing the Indian President. His cavalcade stopped upon seeing a lot of guys running near India Gate. Bush rolled down his window and asked a bystander what the heck was going on.

Bystander: It is a marathon race, Sir.
Bush: What do they get from that?
Bystander: The winner gets a prize.
Bush: Then why are the others running?

...and his eyes couldn't stand the pollution. He went to an eye specialist to get his eyes tested and asked, 'Doctor, will I be able to read after wearing glasses?'

'Yes, of course,' reassured the doctor, 'Why not?'

'Oh, great!' said Bush with joy, 'I have been illiterate for so long.'

...and was brought to court on charges of drunken driving. (It had to happen.) Just before the trial there was a commotion in the gallery. The judge pounded the gavel on his table and shouted, 'Order, order!' Bush immediately responded, 'Thank you, your honour, I'll have a Scotch and soda.'

...and decided to buy low-fi Indian color TVs for the kids back home.

'Do you have color TVs?' Bush asked the saleswoman.

'Sure,' she replied.

'Give me a green one, please.'

...and wanted to take Dick Cheney on a trip to see Bombay High Fields. Both went to the New Delhi Railway Station.

'Can I take this train to Mumbai?,' queried Cheney. 'No,' answered the Railways man.

'Can I?' asked Bush.

Senior Junior II

'If a frog had wings, he wouldn't hit his tail on the ground. Too hypothetical.'

–George Bush Senior

'Families is where our nation finds hope, where wings take dream.'

–George W. Bush

A typical scene in the US: Laura Bush is reading about the discovery of America in a book of history. She comes across the note: Columbus 1492. 'What could it

mean?' she asks her husband. He replies 'Well, it might be his phone number.'

Cheney, Rumsfeld and Bush are asked which technical achievement they consider the greatest. Cheney answers: 'The car—it makes us dynamical.'

Rumsfeld says 'Astronautics technology —it opens up new horizons.'

Bush's answer: ' The vacuum mug. In summer, Laura fills it up with ice tea for me and the tea is kept cool. In winter time, she fills it up with hot coffee and the coffee is kept hot. I wonder how the vacuum mug knows whether it is summer or winter!'

Teacher: What is 5 plus 4?
Bush: 9.
Teacher: What is 4 plus 5?
Bush: Are you trying to fool me? You've just twisted the figure. The answer is 6.

Bush and Laura came to a movie hall and bought two tickets.

A few minutes later, Bush returned and bought two more.

After a short interval, he appeared a third time and offered to pay for two more. The ticket-seller opened the little door in the glass, bowed respectfully and spoke up.

'Sir, didn't you just buy four tickets just a little while ago?' she asked. 'Yes,' replied Bush. 'But there's some fool at the gate who keeps tearing them up.'

Writing on the Wall

George Bush was walking down the reconstructed Twin Towers in Manhattan. He paused to read the graffiti on the wall.

'You are an ass for reading this.'

Bush sat down and began mulling. After he had thought for an hour, he erased the graffiti and wrote back.

'You are an ass for writing this.'

☺

Before they were married, Laura Bush asked George W. 'Georgie, when we get engaged will you give me a ring?

'Sure,' replied George W. 'What's your phone number?'

☺

Examination time

Bush once sat for a university entrance examination. The entire paper consisted of simple Yes/No-type questions. Bush took his seat in the examination hall, fortified himself with a big swig, stared at the question paper for five minutes, and then in a fit of inspiration took his wallet out, removed a coin and started tossing the coin and marking the answer sheet.

Heads meant Y and Tails N.

Within half an hour, Bush was all done whereas the rest of the class was sweating it out.

During the last few minutes, he was again desperately throwing the coin, swearing and sweating. An invigilator, alarmed, approached him and asked what was going on.

'I finished the exam in half an hour, the future US President proudly said. 'But', he added, 'I am having a tough time rechecking my answers.'

Bush goes to the doctor for a check up.

The doctor says, 'I'm sorry, but I have to tell you that you have a problem in your brain. Your brain has two parts, one left and one right. Now, the left part has nothing right in it and the right part has nothing left in it.'

A reporter cornered George W. Bush at a press conference:

'Many say the only reason why you would be elected for President is due to the enormous power and influence of your father.'

'That notion is ridiculous!' mocked George Jr. 'It doesn't matter how powerful the man is. He can only vote once!'

The Bet

George Dubya and Dick Cheney are watching the 6 o'clock news one evening. Cheney bets Dubya $50 that the man in the lead story, who is threatening to jump from a 40-story building, will jump. 'I'll take that bet,' Dubya replied.

A few minutes later, the newscaster breaks in to report that the man had, indeed, jumped from the building. Cheney, feeling sudden guilt for having bet on such an incident, turns to Dubya and tells him that he does not need to pay the $50.

'No, a bet's a bet,' Dubya replied, 'I owe you $50 dollars.'

Cheney, feeling even more guilty, replied, 'No, you don't understand, I saw the 3:00 edition, so I knew how it was going to turn out.'

'That's okay,' said Dubya, 'I saw it earlier too, but I didn't think he'd do it again.'

The Phantom Car

Bush was driving on a lonely stretch of road somewhere on the West. It was pitch dark and not a soul was to be seen when his car broke down.

Having no choice, Bush started walking on the side of the road, hoping to get a lift to the nearest human habitation. The night rolled on and it was cold and he was

shivering.... Suddenly, Bush saw a car coming towards him.

It slowed and then stopped next to him—without thinking Bush opened the car's door and jumped in. Seated in the back, Bush leant forward to thank the person who had saved him when he realized: There was nobody behind the wheel!!

The car began moving slowly, straight up to a curve ahead. Scared almost to death Bush prayed, begging the Lord for his life. His prayers were granted: Just before he hit the curve, a hand appeared through the car window and moved the wheel.

The car made the curve safely and continued on the road to the next bend. Bush, paralyzed in terror, watched how the hand appeared every time they reached a curve and moved the steering wheel just enough to get the car around each bend.

Finally, Bush saw lights ahead.

Gathering his courage Bush wrenched open the door of the car, scrambled out and ran as hard as he could towards the lights. It was a small town. He went to a motel and asked for a stiff shot. And then started telling whoever was in the motel about the horrible experience he'd just been through.

A silence enveloped everybody when they realized that Bush wasn't drunk, and was really frightened. So they gave him more hooch.

Just then two guys walked into the motel, and one said to the other: 'Look, Adam that's the jerk that got in the car when we were pushing it.'

Why has Bush got a clean conscience?— Because he has never made use of it!

Bush asks Laura, 'Now be honest—what kind of man do you prefer: A beautiful one or a smart one?'
Laura answers, 'Neither ... I only love you, George!'

☺

Fuzzy Logic

George W. was preparing for his MBA exams. He could understand everything apart from the section on Logic. One day when he was burning the midnight oil, Cheney came home.

Cheney: How is your preparation?

Bush: Every thing is OK, but I don't dig the Logic section.

Cheney: Logic is very easy.

Bush: Can you give me an example?

Bush: Ok. Do you have a fish pot in your house?

Bush: Yes.

Cheney: Logically, there will be water in it.

Bush: Yes.

Cheney: Logically, there will be fish in it.

Bush: Yes.

Cheney: Logically, someone will be feeding the fish.

Bush: Yes.

Cheney: I guess that your wife will be feeding the fish.

Bush: Yes.

Cheney: So, *logically*, you are married.

Bush: YES.

Cheney: So, logically, you are not homosexual.

Bush was very glad that he understood logic.

Next day he saw Rumsfeld, who was also preparing for an MBA.

Bush: How is your MBA preparation?

Rumsfeld: Everything is fine except for the logic.

Bush: Oh, logic is easy; Cheney told me all about it yesterday.

Rumsfeld: What do you say about showing me how?

Bush: Do you have a fish pot in your house?

Rumsfeld: No. I eat Sushi in restaurants.

Bush: Then you are a homosexual!

'If this were a dictatorship, it would be a heck of a lot easier—so long as I'm the dictator.'

Senior Junior III

'If a frog had wings, he wouldn't hit his tail on the ground. Too hypothetical.'
–George Bush Senior

'Families is where our nation finds hope, where wings take dream.'
–George W. Bush

Bush's White House Tour

Before the inauguration, George W. was invited to a 'get acquainted' tour of the White House. After drinking several glasses of iced tea, he asked President Clinton if he could use his personal bathroom. He was astonished to see that the President had a solid gold urinal!

That afternoon, George W. told his wife, Laura, about the urinal. 'Just think,' he said, 'when I am President, I'll have my own personal gold urinal!'

Later, when Laura had lunch with Hilary at her tour of the White House, she told Hilary how impressed George had been with his discovery of the fact that, in the President's private bathroom, the President had a gold urinal.

That evening, Bill and Hilary were getting ready for bed. Hilary turned to Bill and said, 'Well, I found out who peed in your saxophone.'

☺

Child: What is the White House like?

Bush: It's white.

☹

The good news is Bush is a man of his word—the bad news is no one can find the word in the dictionary.

☺

Bush insists that deep down he is Green. 'It's true I want nothing more than to see the earth completely covered with beautiful plants—steel plants, oil plants, nuclear plants . . .

Someone asked Bush why he thought the Cold War had ended. He replied nervously, 'Global Warming?'

Dubya met with advisers to talk about germ warfare. 'What do you want us to do about weapons which use chemicals from bacteria?' Bush replied instantly, 'Easy. Go to the Balkans and bomb those freaking Bacterians till they stop supplying them.'

Bush went to a fish restaurant and ordered Salman Rushdie.

'See, we love—we love freedom. That's what they didn't understand. They hate things; we love things. They act out of hatred; we don't seek revenge, we seek justice out of love.'

George Bush and Dick Cheney are having lunch at a diner near the White House. Cheney orders the 'Heart Healthy' salad. Bush leans over to the waitress and says, 'Honey, could I have a quickie?'

Horrified, she says, 'Mr President, I thought your administration would bring a new era of moral rectitude to the White House. Now I see I was wrong.' And she marches off.

Cheney leans over and says, 'George, I think it's pronounced "Quiche".'

Dick Cheney took Dubya to see an art house movie in New York. After, Dick asked George, ‘Did you follow the subtext?’ George said, ‘No, I came in the limo as usual.’

Bushier

Jokes Bush Reads

An Iraqi news editor got 20 years in prison for calling Saddam a fool.

Five years for the scandal and fifteen for revealing a state secret!

A brain tumor patient with end-stage disease was informed that he needed an immediate brain transplant operation. The surgeon told him, 'You can have an Indian brain for $10,000 dollars or an American's for $25,000 dollars or I can give you 10 grammes of an Iraqi's brain for $100,000 dollars.' The patient asked, 'Why is the Iraqi's brain so much more expensive than the others?' 'Well,' replied the surgeon, 'we have to go through a lot of Iraqis to find 10 grammes of brain.'

How do you save a drowning Iraqi?
Take the Marine's foot off his head!

Iraq just got its new Arab fighter planes and sent a squadron of pilots there for training.

'Ok, this one is easy to fly', said the trainer, 'even you fools should be able to operate it!'

'You press this button to go up, this one to go left and this one for turning right!'

'But how do we come down?' asked the squadron leader.

'Oh,' said the trainer, 'leave that to the US Air Force!'

A woman and her little girl were visiting the grave of the little girl's grandmother. On their way through the cemetery back to

the car, the little girl asked, 'Mommy, do they ever bury two people in the same grave?'

'Of course not, dear,' replied the mother. 'Why would you think that?'

'The tombstone back there said: "Here lies an Iraqi and an intelligent man."'

'The war on terror involves Saddam Hussein because of the nature of Saddam Hussein, the history of Saddam Hussein, and his willingness to terrorize himself.'

Abdullah, the Afghan, went to JFK Airport to buy his ticket back home. At the counter, he found that he was 10 cents short of the fare.

Having no other way out, he turned to all the other passengers and begged: 'Will someone please give me 10 cents? I badly want to go back and meet my Abba and Ammi again!'

'Here,' said an American, reaching into his wallet and handing him ten dollars, 'keep the change and take nine of your countrymen with you!'

Bush and Powell Plan World War III

Bush and Powell were sitting in a bar. A guy walked in and asked the barman, 'Isn't that Bush and Powell?'

The barman said, 'Yep, that's them.'

So the guy walked over and said, 'Hello. What are you guys doing?'

Bush said, 'We're planning World War III.'

The guy asked, 'Really? What's going to happen?'

Bush said, 'Well, we're going to kill 10

million Iraqis and one bicycle repairman.'

The guy exclaimed, 'Why are you gonna kill a bicycle repairman?'

Bush turned to Powell and said, 'See, I told you no one would worry about the 10 million Iraqis!'

☺

The discovery that Bush's resting heart rate is 43 has led some observers to speculate that this is the first time we've had a president with a heart rate that matches his IQ.

☺

Asked by his teacher to compare three US presidents, Johnny thought for a moment and said: 'Well, George Washington couldn't tell a lie. Richard Nixon couldn't tell the truth. And George W. Bush can't tell the difference.'

A British doctor says, 'Medicine in my country is so advanced that we can take a kidney out of one man and put it in another and have him looking for work in six weeks.' A German doctor says, 'That's nothing, we can take a lung out of one person and put it in another and have him looking for work in four weeks.' The American doctor, not to be outdone, says, 'You guys are way behind. We just took a man with no brain out of Texas, put him in the White House, and now half the country is looking for work and the other half is preparing for war.'

'I was proud the other day when both Republicans and Democrats stood with me in the Rose Garden to announce their support for a clear statement of purpose: you disarm, or we will.'

Three surgeons from Texas talk about progress in surgery while playing golf. One of them says, 'I am the best surgeon in this state. A pianist had lost 7 fingers in an accident and I all mended them, and 8 month later, he gave a private concert for the Queen of England.' The second surgery replies, 'That's nothing. A young man had lost both his arms as well as both his legs and after I mended them, he won a gold medal in the Olympics.' The third one says 'You are amateurs! Some years ago, a man—being totally high due to cocaine and alcohol—rode into a passing train. All that was left were the horse's but and the cowboy's hat. Today, he is the President of this country!'

☺

Somewhere in the US: A car driver is stuck in a traffic jam when suddenly, someone is knocking on the window. He opens the window and asks: 'What's the matter?'

'Terrorists have abducted President Bush. They demand a ransom of $10 million, otherwise they are going to pour fuel on him and set him on fire. Now we are moving from car to car for the purpose of collecting.'

'And how much do people give on an average?'

'Well, about 5 litres...'

Bush Solves a Puzzle

His closest advisors came to visit Dubya at the White House one evening and found him slamming down beers and whooping it up. They were astonished since he had given up drinking years ago. When asked why he was off the wagon, Dubya replied that he was celebrating finishing a jigsaw

puzzle. They smiled and told him that wasn't much of an accomplishment. 'Ah, but you're wrong. I did it in record time.' When asked what that record was, he replied that he had finished it after only 6 months. Again, they told him that wasn't that great. 'Oh yeah?' said the commander in chief, 'Well the box says 3-5 YEARS!'

'We've tripled the amount of money—I believe it's from $50 million up to $195 million available.'

Deer Hunting

George W. Bush and Dan Quayle where returning from hunting. The two were dragging their dead deer back to their car. Another hunter approached pulling his along too.

'Hey, I don't want to tell you how to do

something...but I can tell you that it's much easier if you drag the deer in the other direction. Then the antlers won't dig into the ground.'

After the third hunter left, the two decided to try it.

A little while later George W. said to Dan Quayle, 'You know, that guy was right. This is a lot easier!'

'Yeah,' George W. added, 'but we're getting farther away from the truck....'

'It would be a mistake for the United States Senate to allow any kind of human cloning to come out of that chamber.'

Bob Packwood, Dick Cheney and George Dubya Bush go into a bar. Packwood orders first. 'I'll have a B and C.' The bartender asks, 'What is a B and C?' 'Bourbon and Coke,' Packwood says.

Cheney orders. 'And, I'll have a G and T.' The bartender asks, 'What's a G and T?' 'Gin and tonic,' Cheney replies. Dubya wants to be cute, too. He says, 'I'll have a 15.' 'OK,' the bartender asks, 'What's a 15?' Dubya says, 'A 7 and 7.'

It's all Japanesian to Bush

When he was a Texas businessman, George Bush went to Japan and arrived at his hotel in the heart of a major Japanese city. He arranged to have a beautiful Geisha to be his companion for the night. The woman arrives, and is more beautiful and sensual than he had imagined. He takes her with unbridled lust. During the act, Bush hears his partner cry out many times, *'Sung Wha! Sungh Wha!'* 'That must be Japanese for "terrific",' Bush tells himself. 'I can tell from the way she's thrashing around that she's never been had like this before.'

The next morning, Bush has an appointment with two important Japanese business associates to play golf. Naturally, he wants to impress the men with his friendliness and goodwill, so when the older gentleman makes a hole in one, Bush shouted, *'Sung Wha! Sung Wha!'*

The Japanese turns, eyebrows raised in surprise, 'Wrong hole? What do you mean, wrong hole?'

'The problem with the French is that they don't have a word for *entrepreneur.'* —Dubya to British Prime Minister Tony Blair

When Bush worked in NASA

The epitome of Space Research, NASA, sometimes has scientists who think too much. One of them, before he became President, was our own Bushy. Here's a simple example of his extremely creative powers (Thank God, Clinton was not there).

Bush received reports from NASA astronauts that their pens would not write in space. Ball points, fountain pens, even quills, nothing worked! So he contacted the people who had supplied the pens and made money available for the production of a pen, which would write in space. Eventually, thousands of dollars later, a suitable pen was produced, incorporating a small gas filled cylinder which propelled the ink out of the pen. It worked both in space and underwater. Bush had solved the problem, albeit at great expense. Many years later, when co-operation with the Russians was established, Bush asked his

NASA counterpart who worked in space research how the Russians had solved the problem. There was no problem, he said, we used a pencil.

'In other words, I don't think people ought to be compelled to make the decision which they think is best for their family.'

From the Bush war files

How do you stop an Iraqi tank ?
Shoot the men who are pushing it.

How do you disable an Iraqi tank ?
Hide the wind-up key.

How do you disable Iraqi missiles?
Cut the rubber band.

Have you ever seen Iraqi war heroes ?
Neither has Iraq.

Did you hear about the other latest Iraqi invention?
The new automatic parachutes: they open on impact.

How do you sink an Iraqi battleship?
Put it in oil.

Did you hear about the 747 jet which crashed into a cemetery in Baghdad?
The Iraqi officials have so far recovered 3000 bodies.

Did you hear about the Iraqi admiral who had asked to be buried at sea?
Five Iraqi sailors died digging his grave.

Did you hear about the shutdown of the Baghdad National Library ?
Somebody stole the book.

You're locked in a room with Saddam Hussein, Adolf Hitler, and Stalin. You have a gun with two bullets. What do you do?

Shoot Saddam Hussein twice to make sure he's dead.

What's brown and black and looks great on Saddam?

A Doberman.

How can you tell when an Iraqi soldier is lying?

His lips are moving.

What do you have when an Iraqi is buried up to his neck in sand?

Not enough sand.

Did you hear about the terrorist that hijacked a 747 full of Iraqis?

He threatened to release one every hour if his demands weren't met.

Puzzled President

Cheney gets a call from his 'boss', W.

'I've got a problem,' says W.

'What's the matter?' asks Cheney.

'Well, you told me to keep busy in the Oval Office, so, I got a jigsaw puzzle, but it's too hard. None of the pieces fit together and I can't find any edges.'

'What's it a picture of?' asks Cheney.

'A big rooster,' replies W.

'All right,' sighs Cheney, 'I'll come over and have a look.'

So he leaves his office and heads over to the Oval Office. W points at the jigsaw on his desk.

Cheney looks at the desk and then turns to W and says, 'For crying out loud, Georgie —put the corn flakes back in the box.'

'The great thing about America is everybody should vote.'

Kofi Anan asks Bush, 'What evidence do you have that Iraq has got mass destruction weapons?'

Dubya replies, 'We've kept the receipts.'

Senior Junior I

'When I need a little advice about Saddam Hussein, I turn to country music.'

–George Bush Senior

'We cannot let terrorists and rogue nations hold this nation hostile or hold our allies hostile.'

–George W. Bush

Bush and Saddam

Saddam Hussein and President George W. Bush meet up in Baghdad for the first round of talks in a new peace process.

When George sits down, he notices 3 buttons on the side of Saddam's chair.

They begin talking. After about 5 minutes, Saddam presses the first button.

A boxing glove springs out of a box on the desk and punches Bush in the face. Confused, Bush carries on talking as Saddam laughs.

A few minutes later the second button is pressed. This time a big boot comes out and kicks Bush in the shin. Again Saddam laughs, and again Bush carries on talking, not wanting to put off the bigger issue of peace between the 2 countries. But when the third button is pressed and another boot comes out and kicks Bush in the privates, he's finally had enough, knowing that he can't do much else but say 'I'm going back home!' he tells the Iraqi. 'We'll finish these talks in two weeks!'

Two weeks pass and Saddam flies to the United States for talks. As the 2 men sit down, Hussein notices 3 buttons on Bush's chair and prepares himself for the American's revenge.

They begin talking and as Saddam is uncooperative, Bush presses the first button. Saddam ducks, but nothing happens. Bush snickers.

A few seconds later, as Hussein continues his belligerence, Bush presses the second button. Saddam jumps up, but again nothing happens. Bush roars with laughter.

As things progress, the third button is pressed, Saddam jumps up again, and again nothing happens. Bush falls on the floor in a fit of hysterics.

'Forget this,' says Saddam. 'I'm going back to Baghdad!'

Bush says through tears of laughter, 'What Baghdad?'

Rumsfeld has invited Bush and Rice to admire his newest high-tech purchase: a

pool which is filled automatically with whatever stuff you call out.

For demonstration, Rumsfeld jumps from the jumping tower first, calling out 'champagne!' and the pool immediately fills with the noble liquid.

It is Rice's turn next and, jumping off the tower, she shouts 'milk and honey' on which she has a bath like Cleopatra.

Then Bush climbs the tower and, about to jump, he stumbles and falls down—calling out 'shit!'

The Pope has announced that he will take part in the hearings of Bush's cabinet—he has promised to be present wherever there's the greatest misery.

Bush's councillors have summoned him to a test of his political and geographical knowledge to prevent further disgraces. They ask him, 'How are the inhabitants of Iraq called?' Dubya answers, 'How could I know? There must be millions of them!'

Senior Junior II

'High tech is potent, precise, and in the end, unbeatable. The truth is, it reminds a lot of people of the way I pitch horseshoes. Would you believe some of the people? Would you believe our dog? Look, I want to give the high-five symbol to high tech.'

–George Bush Senior

'Will the highways on the Internet become more few?'

–George W. Bush

Eyes Wide Shut

Dubya is out jogging one morning and notices a little boy holding a box. Curious, he runs over to the child and says, 'What's in the box kid?'

The little boy says, 'Kittens, they're brand new kittens.'

Dubya laughs and says, 'What kind of kittens?'

'Republicans,' the child says.

'Oh that's cute,' Dubya says and runs off.

A couple of days later Dubya is running with Dick Cheney and he spies the same boy with his box.

Dubya tells Dick, 'You gotta check this out' and they jog over to the boy. Dubya says, 'Look in the box Dick, isn't that cute? Hey kid tell my friend Dick what kind of kittens they are.'

The boy replies, 'They're Democrats.'

'Whoa!', Dubya says, 'I came by here the other day and you said they were Republicans. What's up?'

'Well,' the kid says, 'Their eyes are open now.

How did George W. Bush prove his ignorance?

He failed a DNA test.

'People say, how can I help on this war against terror? How can I fight evil? You can do so by mentoring a child, by going into a shut-in's house and say I love you.'

First Draft of Bush's Inaugural Address

My fellow Armenians,

As I stand here today, looking out over this magnificent viagra, I think we can agree that the past is over. Our country is ready for a fresh, bipolar approach.

I want to bring America together. We are the hill shining on a city, and each of us can get to the top if we set our feet to it... Americans have made their decision. They don't need sympathy; they need ablutions. We need to move beyond the petty armadilloes.

Politics doesn't have to be the way it is today. We can make the pie higher. A high pie lets everyone put food on their family and their family on the table. . .

The purpose of prosperity is to make sure the American dream touches every killing heart. Progress can be slow; you measure it in inches and feet, not miles or kilograms. Or cantilevers. I worked in Texas by common sense and plain dozing. I got on with small business, because I was one myself. I'm less now. But I'm also more. We are all less and more. More or less. And I believe we must match our compassionate hearts to our preservative minds.

I know you would rather be watching TV, and so would I, so I will draw to a confusion. My message is: I will get things done. I will inspire and untie. I will appeal to people's better angles. I will prove that politics can be bigger than you ever thought possible. We will trust the people we serve, and serve the people we trust. Together, we can do what needs to be done to preserve this great bastard of freedom.

Thank you, and God help America.

Beating about the **Bush**

During Bush's air force times:

Tower: You have traffic at 10 o'clock, 6 miles!

Bush: Give me another hint; I've got a digital watch.

George W. Bush is sitting in a hotel lobby, planning his speech to a group of businessmen, when a little man walks up to him. 'Excuse me, Mr. Bush, but my name is Steve Case, and I'm here with an extremely important client tonight. We're going to see your speech tonight, and it would be a great help to me if, when we walk by, you could impress him by saying, "Hello, Steve".'

Bush agrees, and five minutes later, the little man walks by, deep in conversation with his client.

Bush came up and said, 'Hello, Steve.'

The little man says, 'F**k off, Bush! I'm in a meeting,' and walks on.

Three brothers Neil, Jeb and Dub, were stumbling home late one night and found themselves on the road that led past the old graveyard.

'Come have a look over here,' says Neil, 'It's Obidiah Jones' grave, God bless his soul, he lived to the ripe old age of 87.'

'That's nothing,' says Jeb, 'here's one named Butch Smith. It says here that he was 95 when he died.'

Just then, Dub yells out, 'But here's a fella that died when he was 145 years old!'

'What was his name?' asks Neil.

Dub lights a match to see what else is written on the stone marker, and exclaims, 'Miles, from Austin.'

'Let me tell you my thoughts about tax relief. When your economy is kind of ooching along, it's important to let people have more of their own money.'

A researcher called G. W. Bush at his house in Austin.

G.W. was sleeping in late and was awakened by the call.

He was half-asleep when he answered the phone.

Researcher: Excuse me, sir. I'm conducting a survey

G.W. Bush: Questions? No political questions.

Researcher: Political, sir?

G.W. Bush: Do you know who you are calling?

Researcher: We call numbers at random, sir. May I ask . . .

G.W. Bush: What is this about?

Researcher: We are asking people do they think COKE beats PEPSI.

G.W. BUSH: I've never tried Pepsi. Is that a new thing?

'One year ago today, the time for excuse-making has come to an end.'

What did Bush get out of Yale University?

He got out of studying, he got out of exams—but mainly he got out of his skull.

☺

'We need an energy bill that encourages consumption.'

☹

Bush was in Italy on a State visit when Berlusconi said, 'Tomorrow, George, we're taking you to the Leaning Tower of Pisa.' Dubya asked 'Why? Don't you have a Domino's pizza?'

☺

'Now, we talked to Joan Hanover. She and her husband, George, were visiting with us. They are near retirement—retiring—in the process of retiring, meaning they're very smart, active, capable people who are retirement age and are retiring.'

Famous Last Words

Bill Clinton, Al Gore, and George W. Bush were set to face a firing squad in a small Central American country. Bill Clinton was the first one placed against the wall and just before the order was given he yelled out, 'Earthquake!' The firing squad fell into a panic and Bill jumped over the wall and escaped in the confusion.

Al Gore was the second one placed against the wall. The squad was reassembled and Al pondered what he had just witnessed. Again before the order was given Al yelled out, 'Tornado!' Again the squad fell apart and Al slipped over the wall.

The last person, George W. Bush, was placed against the wall. He was thinking, 'I see the pattern here, just scream out something about a disaster and hop over the wall.' He confidently refused the blindfold as the firing squad was reassembled. As the rifles were raised in his direction he grinned from ear to ear and yelled, 'Fire!'

'When Iraq is liberated, you will be treated, tried and persecuted as a war criminal.'

Senior Junior I

'I don't want to get, you know, here
we are close to the election—
sounding a knell of overconfidence
that I don't feel.'

–George Bush Senior

'I don't know whether I'm going to
win or not. I think I am. I do know
I'm ready for the job. And, if not,
that's just the way it goes.'

–George W. Bush

George W. Bush's Intelligence Quiz

While visiting England, George W. Bush is invited to tea with the Queen. He asks her what her leadership philosophy is. She says that it is to surround herself with intelligent people. He asks how she knows if they're intelligent.

'I do so by asking them the right questions,' says the Queen. 'Allow me to demonstrate.'

She phones Tony Blair and says, 'Mr. Prime Minister. Please answer this question: Your mother has a child, and your father has a child, and this child is not your brother or sister. Who is it?'

Tony Blair responds, 'It's me, ma'am.'

'Correct. Thank you and good-bye, sir,' says the Queen. She hangs up and says, 'Did you get that, Mr. Bush?'

'Yes, ma'am. Thanks a lot. I'll definitely be using that!'

Upon returning to Washington, he decides he'd better put the Chairman of the

Senate Foreign Relations Committee to the test. He summons Jesse Helms to the White House and says, 'Senator Helms, I wonder if you can answer a question for me.'

'Why, of course, sir. What's on your mind?'

'Uh, your mother has a child, and your father has a child, and this child is not your brother or your sister. Who is it?'

Helms hems and haws and finally asks, 'Can I think about it and get back to you?' Bush agrees, and Helms leaves. He immediately calls a meeting of other senior senators, and they puzzle over the question for several hours, but nobody can come up with an answer. Finally, in desperation, Helms calls Colin Powell at the State Department and explains his problem.

'Now look here Colin Powell, your mother has a child, and your father has a child, and this child is not your brother, or your sister. Who is it?' Powell answers immediately, 'It's me, of course.'

Much relieved, Helms rushes back to The White House and exclaims, 'I know the answer, sir! I know who it is! It's Colin Powell!' And Bush replies, 'Wrong, you dumb ass, it's Tony Blair!'

'There's an old saying in Tennessee—I know it's in Texas, probably in Tennessee—that says, fool me once, shame on—shame on you. Fool me—you can't get fooled again.'

Bush isn't brilliant at languages. In his English class at Adover the teacher asked, 'George, what's the best way to end a sentence?' George thought for a minute and smiled hopefully, 'The electric chair.'

What's the difference between Bush and *War and Peace*?

War and Peace is thick but you don't want to put it down.

'The Holocaust was an obscene period in our nation's history. I mean in this century's history. But we all lived in this century. I didn't live in this century.'

Senior Junior II

'To kind of suddenly try to get my hair colored, and dance up and down in a miniskirt or do something, you know, show that I've got a lot of jazz out there and drop a bunch of one-liners, I'm running for the President of the United States... I kind of think I'm a scintillating kind of fellow.'

–George Bush Senior

'Actually, I—this may sound a little
West Texan to you, but I like it.
When I'm talking about—when I'm
talking about myself, and when he's
talking about myself, all of us are
talking about me.'

–George W. Bush

Bush is glad his heavy drinking days are behind him. It was awful having glazed eyes, not being able to speak properly, and looking such an idiot—and the drinking just made it worse.

When George W. Bush went to Rome they asked him what he thought of the Sistine—'Great! I pulled the handle and it flushed just like the ones back in Texas.'

Senior Junior III

'It gets into quota, go into numerical, set numbers for doctors or for, it could go into all kinds of things.'

–George Bush Senior

'What I am against is quotas. I am against hard quotas, quotas they basically delineate based upon whatever. However they delineate, quotas, I think vulcanize society. So I don't know how that fits into what everybody else is saying, their relative positions, but that's my position.'

–George W. Bush

Artificial Intelligence

A lady bought a new Lexus. Cost a bundle. Two days later, she brought it back, complaining that the radio was not working.

'Madam,' said the sales manager, 'the audio system in this car is completely automatic. All you need to do is tell it what you want to listen to, and you will hear exactly that!'

She drove out, somewhat amazed and a little confused. She looked at the radio and said, 'Nelson.' The radio responded, 'Ricky or Willie?' She was astounded. If she wanted Beethoven, that's what she got. If she wanted Nat King Cole, she got it.

She was stopped at a traffic light enjoying *On The Road Again* when the light turned green and she pulled out. Suddenly an enormous sports utility vehicle coming from the street she was crossing sped toward her, obviously not paying attention to the light. She swerved and narrowly missed a collision.

'Idiot!' she yelled and, immediately the radio broadcast, 'Ladies and gentlemen, the President of the United States.'

Bombshell

In her memoirs, Barbara Bush described one of those most embarrassing moments that inevitably occur, even on the most carefully planned of foreign trips. Along with her husband, then the Vice President, Mrs Bush was lunching with Emperor Hirohito at Tokyo's Imperial Palace.

Sitting next to the Emperor, Mrs. Bush found the conversation an uphill task. To all her efforts at verbal engagement, the Emperor would smile and say 'Yes' or 'No,' with an occasional 'Thank You' tossed in for good measure.

Looking around her elegant surroundings, she complimented Hirohito on his official residence.

'Thank you,' he said.

'Is it new?' pressed Mrs. Bush.

'Yes.'

'Was the old palace just so old that it was falling down?' asked Mrs. Bush.

In his most charming, yet regal, matter,

Hirohito replied, 'No, I'm afraid, you bombed it.'

Mrs. Bush turned to her other lunch partner.

☹

What is Bush's traffic policy? Jam today and Jam tomorrow.

☺

On a snowy morning when George W. is on his way to work, he sees that someone has peed into the snow 'Bush is stupid'. He is very angry and tells the Security Chief to come over: 'Find out who has made this mess!'

On the next day the Security Chief returns and reports: 'I've got bad news and even worse news—Which one do you want to hear first?'

Bush decides in favour of the bad news.

'Well, we found the culprit. It's the

Minister of Defence.' Bush is enraged. 'And what's the worse news?'—'It's Laura's handwriting.'

What is the difference between Bush and his government and Washington's psychiatric clinic?—The address and the phone number.

Saddam calls Dubya, 'George, I'm giving you a ring, because I had a strange dream last night: I could see the whole USA and it looked so wonderful and on every house there was a banner saying 'God is Allah and Allah is God'.

'Well,' Bush answers, 'I am glad you're calling, because I had a similar dream last night: I had a view of the whole of Iraq and it looked even more beautiful than before

and was just being completely rebuild and there was a banner on every roof top.'

'What was written on the banners?' Saddam asked.

'I don't know—I don't speak Hebrew.'

After his death, Bush knocks on Heaven's Door, but St Peter rejects him and sends him to hell. A few days later, two little devils ask for entrance permission at the Pearly Gates. The astonished St Peter asks them, 'What are you doing here?' 'Well,' they answer, 'we're the first refugees.'

Putin, Blair and Bush have to jump off a plane because it's about to crash.

Bush jumps off first, draws the line, the lead and his parachute opens.

Putin gets off next, but his parachute

doesn't open and so he is speeding down to earth.

Blair isn't lucky with his parachute, either and soon is overtaking Bush, too—falling down speedily.

Bush is astonished for a moment. Then he loosens the belts of his parachute, thinking: 'All right then, if this is to be a race.'

Senior Junior IV

'We're enjoying sluggish times, and not enjoying them very much.'

–George Bush Senior

'A tax cut is really one of the anecdotes to coming out of an economic illness.'

–George W. Bush

Once George W. Bush and Donald Rusmfeld gave an English exam.

Rumsfeld: How was your exam?

Bush: I only made one mistake.

Rumsfeld: Great, what was the mistake?

Bush: They asked me the plural of think and I thank and thank and thank.

The Bush report card

Politics

Needs to try harder. Apparently thinks manual recount is a Mexican revolutionary.

Foreign languages

See English

English

No one uses the language quite like George.

Maths

Fuzzy. Dubya Bush must remember Pythagoras is not some Grecian towelhead, logarithms are not what lumberjacks do on the dance floor, and algebra is not the little mermaids' underwear.

Hu's on first

George: Condi! Nice to see you. What's happening?

Condi: Sir, I have the report here about the new leader of China.

George: Great. Lay it on me.

Condi: Hu is the new leader of China.

George: That's what I want to know.

Condi: That's what I'm telling you.

George: That's what I'm asking you. Who is the new leader of China?

Condi: Yes.

George: I mean the fellow's name.

Condi: Hu.

George: The guy in China.

Condi: Hu.

George: The new leader of China.

Condi: Hu.

George: The Chinaman!

Condi: Hu is leading China.

George: Now whaddya' asking me for?

Condi: I'm telling you Hu is leading China.

George: Well, I'm asking you. Who is leading China?

Condi: That's the man's name.

George: That's who's name?

Condi: Yes.

George: Will you or will you not tell me the name of the new leader of China?

Condi: Yes, sir.

George: Yassir? Yassir Arafat is in China? I thought he was in the Middle East.

Condi: That's correct.

George: Then who is in China?

Condi: Yes, sir.

George: Yassir is in China?

Condi: No, sir.

George: Then who is?

Condi: Yes, sir.

George: Yassir?

Condi: No, sir.

George: Look, Condi. I need to know the name of the new leader of China. Get me the Secretary General of the U.N. on the phone.

Condi: Kofi?

George: No, thanks.

Condi: You want Kofi?

George: No.

Condi: You don't want Kofi.

George: No. But now that you mention it, I could use a glass of milk. And then get me the U.N.

Condi: Yes, sir.

George: Not Yassir! The guy at the U.N.

Condi: Kofi?

George: Milk! Will you please make the call?

Condi: And call who?

George: Who is the guy at the U.N?

Condi: Hu is the guy in China.

George: Will you stay out of China?!

Condi: Yes, sir.

George: And stay out of the Middle East! Just get me the guy at the U.N.

Condi: Kofi.

George: All right! With cream and two sugars. Now get on the phone.

(Condi picks up the phone.)

Condi: Rice, here.

George: Rice? Good idea. And a couple of egg rolls, too. Maybe we should send some to the guy in China. And the Middle East. Can you get Chinese food in the Middle East?

Nothing Personal, Mr Bush!

Roaming the streets of London during the heyday of protests against the war in Iraq, amidst thousands of anti-war posters and protesters, one of us chanced upon a beggar with a bush in hand and a placard across the chest saying: 'This Bush is for Peace.'

People in authority frequently lend themselves to satire. Occasionally, they play jokes on the world; sometimes they become jokes themselves.

Hence George W. Bush, President of the USA—a perfect candidate—was unanimously elected for this book. (No recounts, please.) Dubya is central to the jokes; he is the spirit of the jokes. As Nietzsche said in an entirely different context, if there was no God we would have had to invent one. Bush, therefore, is as much a product of the collective human imagination as he is the President of the USA.

Did we overlook that while compiling these jokes? Not really. Most of the gags on Dubya are born out of the fact that people like him are very important. (We in India are especially sensitive to such irony; after all sometimes we have had fumble harmers as prime ministers). Others hatch out of Dubya's colorful Texan background: his coke-snorting days, his aborted alcoholic evenings, his dyslexia or his fine quotes: 'More and more of our imports come from overseas' or better still 'The name of the Indian Prime Minister is... no.'

While the book was being produced, the publisher was the only one who reminded the assorted jokers on his payroll that the one they were writing about was the President of the United States. It is also good to remember—for the reader and the writer—that George W. is not George Washington or even Clinton. That immediately takes care of the selection of jokes: so many now—and it's really a pity what with Lewinsky and all—cannot be included.

But what about intelligence? Well, in this age of artificial intelligence, a joke book on Bush is not such a bad idea. And what about common sense, sound logic, sensitivity, fine appreciation? That is what we keep for the rest of our books. This one was for letting off steam—at, for instance, the cultural numbness of those that burnt libraries and rare papyrus manuscripts and walked off with 7000 years of history. As book lovers, how else could we register our protest at the arrogance of the war: the precision bombing got almost every target from the Palestine Hotel and the Baghdad marketplace to the museums in which Babylon still breathed, but missed, rather mysteriously, the oil ministry and Saddam. In its wake, the Weapons of Mass

Destruction (WMDs) too vanished overnight.

From the sidelines, we could only try to draw attention to the Man in Charge of the World. So, enter the cowboy from Texas, a firearm dangling by his side, or (for the more literary-minded), a modern-day Don Quixote tilting at windmills with an Anglo-Saxon Sancho Panza, Tony Blair.

There is also a gallery of fascinating rogues with whom Dubya is associated. We do not mean Dick, Rumsfeld or Powell. We refer instead to the larger-than-life figures like bin Laden and Saddam Hussein. These are the villains amidst whom our hero strides, a special Gillette scimitar in hand and chewing gum in mouth. But none of them would stand an earthly chance of being recorded by history had Bush not immortalized them.

It is rare to find a President who speaks so much and so... well! A lampooner's delight, a cartoonist's dream-come-true, Dubya is our Man of the Millennium (take a bow *Time*) and we must count ourselves fortunate that he came in our lifetime. History will testify one day that he was made for some enterprising publisher's joke book.

Moses was led by the Burning Bush, we were led by the burns Bush left in his wake.

No hard feelings, Mr Bush!